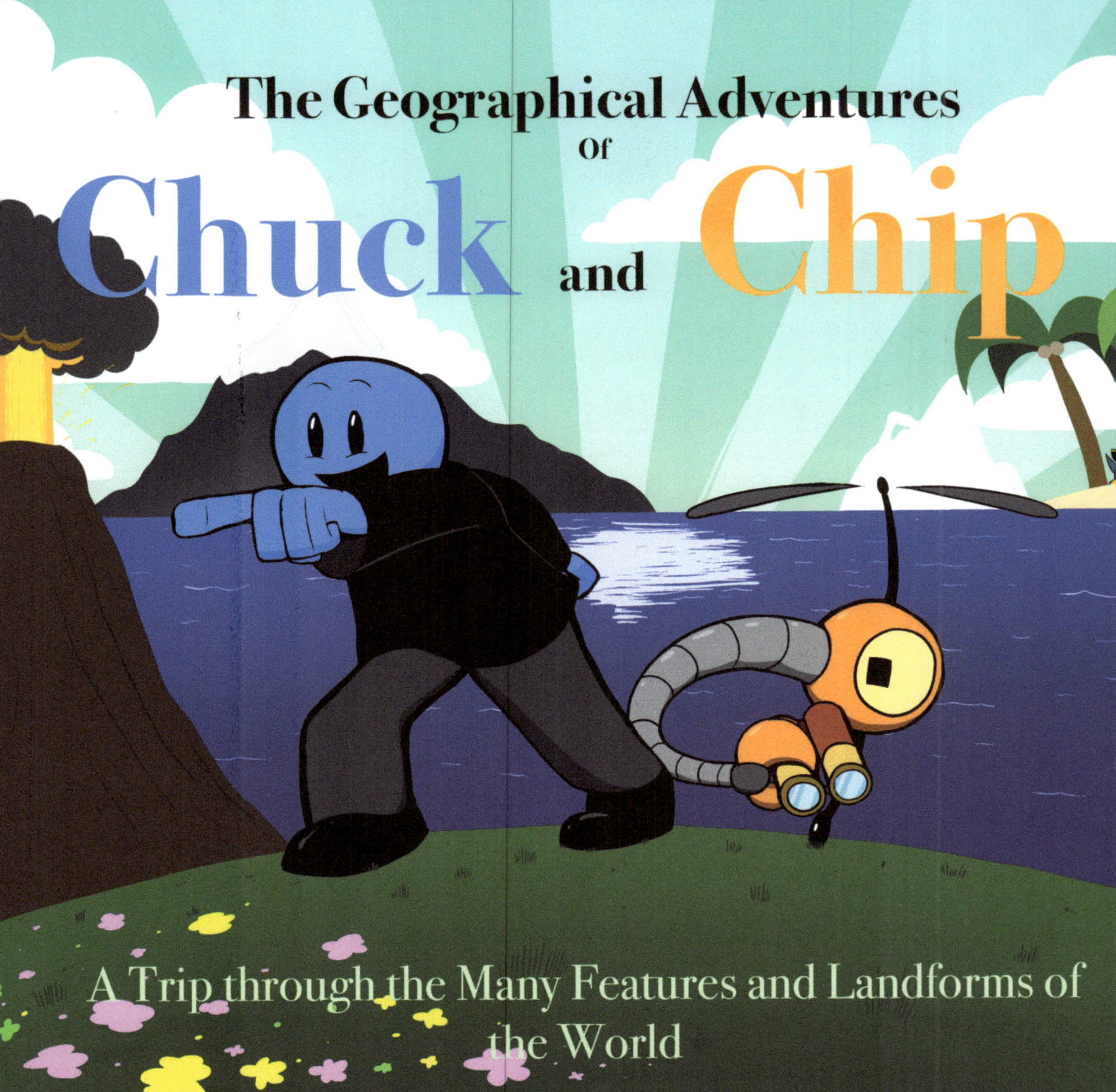

The Geographical Adventures of Chip & Chuck
A TRIP THROUGH THE MANY FEATURES AND LANDFORMS OF THE WORLD

Copyright © 2024 Noah Hudson.

All rights reserved. No part of this book may be used or reproduced by any means, graphic, electronic, or mechanical, including photocopying, recording, taping or by any information storage retrieval system without the written permission of the author except in the case of brief quotations embodied in critical articles and reviews.

The views expressed in this work are solely those of the author and do not necessarily reflect the views of the publisher, and the publisher hereby disclaims any responsibility for them.

iUniverse books may be ordered through booksellers or by contacting:

iUniverse
1663 Liberty Drive
Bloomington, IN 47403
www.iuniverse.com
844-349-9409

Because of the dynamic nature of the Internet, any web addresses or links contained in this book may have changed since publication and may no longer be valid. The views expressed in this work are solely those of the author and do not necessarily reflect the views of the publisher, and the publisher hereby disclaims any responsibility for them.

Any people depicted in stock imagery provided by Getty Images are models, and such images are being used for illustrative purposes only.
Certain stock imagery © Getty Images.

ISBN: 978-1-6632-6234-9 (sc)
ISBN: 978-1-6632-6232-5 (hc)
ISBN: 978-1-6632-6233-2 (e)

Library of Congress Control Number: 2024908109

Print information available on the last page.

iUniverse rev. date: 05/06/2024

The Geographical Adventures
of
Chuck and Chip

By Noah Hudson

About the author
<u>Noah Hudson</u>

Hi, My name is Noah! Like my friends Chuck and Chip, I have traveled all around the world. I like to draw pictures of the places I've been and the things I've seen. Just like Chuck, I've swum with manatees in Florida, visited the castles in Wales and gone crabbing in Delaware.

I've always enjoyed geography, so much that when I was in high school, I taught it to younger children when I had the opportunity.

I understand that lots of people learn best from stories and pictures. So, I thought of making this fun adventure book, to help teach the Earth's geographical features, all while having a fun story too.

Meet the travelers

Chuck Chucklestein

A happy go lucky traveler who likes two things: exploring and making friends with everyone he sees. For Chuck, the more friends in a trip, the better!

The Companion Handyman 1-P
(Chip for short)

Chip is Chuck's travel buddy. He's a worrisome robot, keeping an eye on Chuck in case he wanders into danger. When he does, Chip always pulls him out of danger with his extendible claw arm.

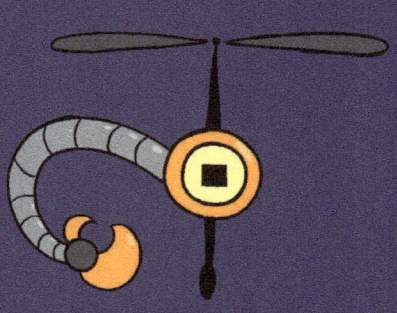

Stop #1
Archipelago

An archipelago is a group of islands clustered together.

Fun Fact

Archipelagos aren't just seen in oceans. They can also be seen in fresh water too!

High altitude

Low altitude

Stop #2
<u>Altitude</u>

Altitude is the height or point something is above sea level or ground level.

Stop #3
Atoll

An atoll is a ring of islands with a lagoon in the center. Usually there are traces of a volcano that sunk into the water.

Fun fact

The islands of an atoll are made of the coral reef that used to be around a volcano!

3

Stop #4
Arm

An arm is a narrow inlet of water stretching out of a larger body of water, such as a lake or ocean.

Stop #5
Bank

A bank is the land along the side of a river.

Stop #6
<u>Basin</u>

A basin is a bowl-shaped depression or dip in the Earth's surface. Some basins have water on the bottom of them, such as river basins or drainage basins.

Fun fact

The basin in the image on the left is a river basin.

Stop #7
<u>Bayou</u>

A bayou is a marshy, slow-moving lake or river outlet with usually brackish water.

Stop #8
<u>Bay</u>

A bay is an inlet of the sea where the land curves inward. It's not a lake, as it's still connected to the ocean.

Stop #9
Beach

Everyone's favorite (or at least my favorite) place to go. A beach is a place where the land meets the sea/ocean.

Fun Fact

Not all beaches have white sand. Some have black sand. Others may have none, with only a stone floor.

Stop #10
Bluff

A bluff is a steep shoreline slope made from sediment. It's caused by heavy erosion from the sea.

Stop #11
<u>Bog</u>

A bog is a freshwater wetland with wet spongy ground made from peat, which is old dead plant matter.

Stop #12
Brink

A brink is the slope of a high-standing area such as a cliff.

Stop #13
Canal

A canal is a man-made waterway commonly used as a boat passage, or a way to transfer water.

Stop #14
Canyon

A canyon is a deep gorge in the land, usually caused by a river, which can be seen in the center of the canyon.

Stop #15
Cape

A cape is a high point of land that sticks out into a lake, river, or ocean.

Fun Fact

Unlike a peninsula (which we'll get to eventually), a cape is much narrower and smaller.

Stop #16
Cave

A cave is an opening (usually natural) found in things such as hills, mountains, or cliffs.

Fun Fact

Various wildlife, such as bears and bats, seek refuge in caves.

Stop #17
Cavern

A cavern is a very large chamber, usually deep inside a cave.

Fun Fact

There are creatures that spend their entire lives within caverns. They are completely blind and don't need eyes.

Stop #18
Chasm

A chasm is a deep fissure or crack in the earth, floor, or rock.

Stop #19
Channel

A channel is a length of water that usually connects two larger bodies of water like a sea or large lake. These can also be called straits.

Fun Fact

Some channels might not even have water. There are channels that may have lava!

Stop #20
Cinder Cone

A cinder cone is a mound of ash piled up around a volcano. The ash makes a cone shape around its central vent, hence the name.

Fun Fact

Cinder cones can come in various shapes, like domes. The shape depends on the viscosity of the lava.

Stop #21
Cliff

A cliff is the steep rock face at the edge of an elevated piece of land.

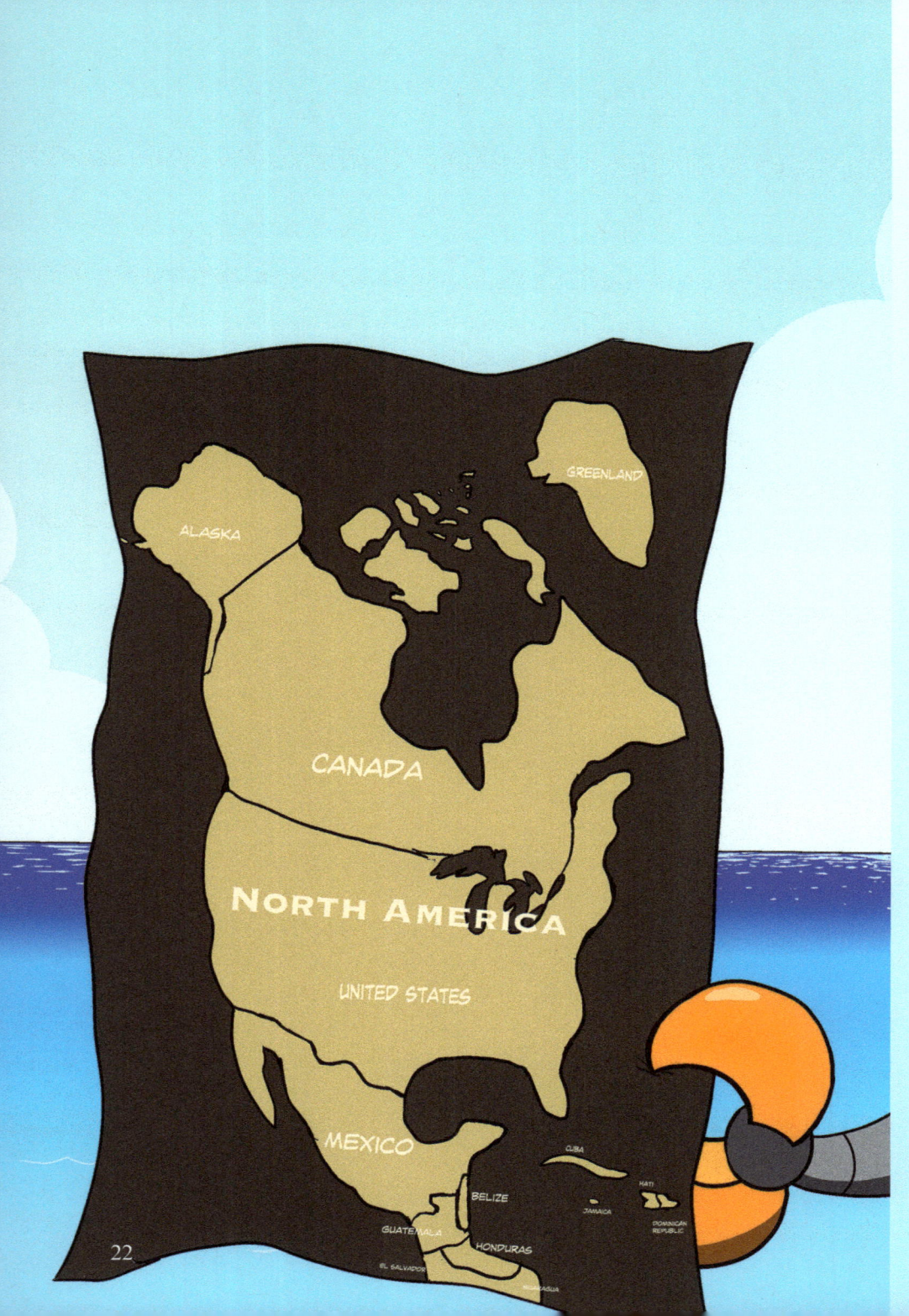

Stop #22
Continent & Country

A continent is a large expanse of land usually housing many countries.

A country is a nation with its own government, located on a continent.

Stop #23
Continental Shelf

A continental shelf is the area of the seabed where the water is shallow compared to the rest of the ocean. It's usually a part of the continent it borders.

Fun Fact

The edge of the continental shelf that dips into the deeper ocean is known as the continental slope.

Stop #24
Cove

A cove is a concave inlet like a bay, with a narrow entrance. They are usually circular in appearance with a lagoon in the center. A lagoon is a semi-deep reservoir of water almost disconnected from the ocean.

Fun Fact

A cove can also mean a cave.

Stop #25
<u>Crags</u>

Crags are jagged and steep rock faces or cliffs.

Stop #26
Crater

A crater is a large bowl-shaped cavity in the earth. They are often created by things like meteorites and volcanos.

Fun Fact

Craters can also be made from manmade explosions.

Stop #27
<u>Creek</u>

A creek is a small stream. It can also be a tributary of a larger river. A synonym for a creek is a brook.

Stop #28
Cultivated Land

Cultivated land is land that is used to produce crops and other resources. Farms are cultivated land.

Stop #29
Current

A current is the part of a body (such as air or water) moving continuously in a certain direction.

Fun Fact

A current can also be used to describe a flow of electricity!

Stop #30
<u>Dale</u>

A dale is a wide section of low land that spans between mountains

Fun Fact

The difference between a dale and a valley is that a valley is narrower.

Stop #31
Dam

A dam is a structure that can be either natural or artificial. It is used to block water flow.

Fun Fact

Some manmade dams can even be used to generate hydroelectric power.

Stop #32
Delta

A delta is a natural structure at the mouth of a river where sediment collects to form a bit of land.

Stop #33
Dell

A dell is a small valley found between the trees in a forest. In literature, they are often portrayed as safe havens.

Stop #34
Desert

A desert is a barren area where living conditions are harsh for plants and animals.

Fun Fact

Deserts aren't always sandy. The arctic and some areas of the ocean can be considered deserts.

Stop #35
Dune

A dune is a hill of sand or loose sediment, usually formed by the wind.

Stop #36
Dike

A dike is a slab of rock that cuts into a much larger rock formation in the earth.

Stop #37
Earth

The Earth is the third planet from the sun. It has the perfect conditions to support life. Earth also means dirt or soil.

Stop #38
Fall Line & Elevation

A fall line is a narrow line that marks the separation of an upland region and a plain. An elevation is the distance that land rises from sea level.

Fun Fact

Fall lines sometimes have waterfalls around them due to their elevation.

Stop #39
Estuary

An estuary is a part of the river near the mouth where the tide meets the river. Sometimes there is a sandbar or delta nearby.

Fun Fact

Estuaries are great ecosystems, and many animals use them to grow young or find food.

Stop #40
Field

A field is a large open piece of land.

Fun Fact

Fields can be both natural and artificial. Sometimes fields can be used for sports.

Stop #41
Ford

A ford is a shallow crossable section of a river that can be walked over. This is usually seen in creeks or streams.

41

Stop #42
Fjord

A fjord is a narrow but deep inlet of water between cliffs.

Stop #43
Foothill

Foothills are the lower slopes of mountains, or smaller hills near the base of a much larger mountain or mountain range.

Stop #44
Glacier

A glacier is a large river of ice, made from compaction of snow from mountains or near the poles.

Fun Fact

Glaciers are said to be responsible for cutting into mountains and creating fjords.

Stop #45
Forest

A forest is a dense region covered by trees and undergrowth.

Fun Fact

Forests can vary depending on the types of trees present.

Stop #46
Gorge

A gorge is a narrow, steep valley usually with water flowing rapidly at the bottom.

Stop #47
<u>Gulch</u>

A gulch is a steep ravine.

Fun Fact

A gulch is a synonym for a gorge.

Stop #48
Gulf

A gulf is a large, deep inlet of the sea surrounded by land. It usually has a narrow mouth.

Stop #49
Headland

A headland is a narrow piece of high land that sticks out into the sea.

Stop #50

Hill

A hill is a low rise in the ground. It's not as big as a mountain but it's big enough to be noticed.

Fun Fact

There are many synonyms for these geographical features, like knobs.

Stop #51
Harbor

A harbor is an area that boats go to, whether it be to pick up cargo, drop of passengers, or rest for repairs. In summary, it's a parking lot for boats.

Stop #52

Iceberg

An iceberg is a big piece of ice floating in the ocean.

Fun Fact

Icebergs are much larger underwater. To test this fact, drop a piece of ice in a clear cup of water and see how much of it is underwater!

Stop #53
Island

An island is a piece of land that is surrounded by water.

Fun Fact

The largest island in the world is Australia, which is an entire continent.

Stop #54
Isthmus

An isthmus is a thin strip of land that connects two larger bodies of land together.

Stop #55
<u>Jungle</u>

A jungle is a tropical forest that is overgrown with vegetation and wildlife.

Stop #56
Inlet

An inlet is an indentation in the shore. It is usually an extension of a lake, river, or sea.

Fun Fact

Bays, arms, and coves are all different forms of inlets.

Stop #57
Irrigated Land

Irrigated land is an area of land that is usually fed by water. Irrigation can be achieved naturally by streams or artificially by a sprinkler system.

Fun Fact

Irrigation is often used for agriculture and farming.

Stop #58
Junction

A junction is a point where two things meet. This can be naturally occurring, like two rivers, or something more artificial, like two roads.

Stop #59
Knobs & Knolls

Knobs and knolls are the same. They are both small rounded hills, with knolls being a bit smaller.

Stop #60
Latitude & Longitude

Longitude lines are the grid lines that run north and south on a map. Latitude lines run east to west. Together, they form a grid to help locate specific places.

Stop #61
Lake

Lakes are bodies of water disconnected from sources such as the ocean or the sea.

Fun Fact

The Caspian Sea, despite being called a sea, is actually a lake. It's just a really big one, the biggest lake in the world.

61

Stop #62
Locks

Locks are artificial structures made to lower or raise boats in a canal.

Stop #63
Levee

A levee is a structure that is made to block off water from a specific area. These can occur naturally or be made artificially.

Stop #64
Meadow

A meadow is a piece of grassland often used to grow plants such as flowers or wheat. Most meadows are used for agriculture, but some are decorative.

Stop #65
Marsh

A marsh is an area that is waterlogged most of the time. This is the result of frequent flooding during the wet seasons.

Stop #66
Mesa

A mesa is an isolated flat-topped elevation with steep sides. Mesas usually are found in plains.

Fun Fact

There are many mesas in the Grand Canyon.

Stop #67
Mine

A mine is a man-made entrance dug into the earth to excavate ores such as coal, iron, gold, and diamonds.

Stop #68

Mountain

A mountain is a naturally elevated piece of the earth's surface that is higher than the surrounding ground.

Fun Fact

Unlike a hill, a mountain is very large, large enough to be visible from space.

Stop #69
Mountain Range

A mountain range is a collection of mountains grouped together. If it's a group of singular mountains lined up, it's called a mountain chain instead.

Fun Fact

Mountain ranges are a telltale sign that two of Earth's tectonic plates have collided!

Stop #70

Moor

A moor is a type of large temperate grassland.

Stop #69
Mouth

A mouth is the opening at the end of a river or flowing source, such as a stream or creek.

Stop #72
Natural Resource

Natural resources are any kind of resource found in nature that can be used. Examples are solar power, and oil. Wind, for example, is a natural resource because it can be used to power windmills and sailboats!

Stop #73
Ocean

An ocean is a large expanse of water that spans across the world. It separates continents.

Fun Fact

The ocean is still relatively unexplored.

Stop #74
Peninsula

A peninsula is an inlet of land that sticks out into a body of water. A peninsula is much wider and larger than a cape

Stop #75
Oasis

An oasis is a small area in a desert with fertile land. There usually is a pond of water in the center of an oasis.

Stop #76
Pasture

A pasture is land that is covered in grass and plants suitable for grazing animals.

Stop #77
Piedmont & Pass

A piedmont is the land leading from a flat land to the slope of a mountain. A pass is a gap between two mountains.

Stop #78
Plateau

A plateau is the flat surface of a high-altitude piece of land.

Stop #79
Plain

Plains are vast expanses of flat land with little elevation. They usually occur as lowlands, along valleys.

Stop #80
Pond

A pond is a small body of water that is surrounded by land. They serve as great nesting grounds for wildlife.

Stop #81
Pier

A pier is a long manmade structure made for boats to park and or dispatch.

Stop #82
Rapids

Rapids are parts of a river where water flows the fastest and is the most turbulent.

Safety Fact

Never go down rapids without proper equipment and training.

Stop #83
River

A river is a constantly moving stream of water. Rivers usually start up at higher altitudes in lakes, which are their sources.

Fun fact

Rivers can span the length of a country and beyond, like the Mississippi River or the Nile.

Stop #84

River Mouth

The river mouth is the end of a river. River mouths can connect to the sea, ocean, or even other rivers, making them bigger

Fun fact

Deltas usually form at the mouths of rivers.

Stop #85
Shore

A shore is the land that is next to a body of water.

Fun fact

Many things wash up on shores, like shells, corals, and objects from other parts of the world.

Stop #86
Sandbar

A sandbar is a narrow elevation of sand that usually sticks out of the water. Sandbars are disconnected from the shore.

Fun fact

Sandbars usually appear at river mouths, but they can also appear on beaches.

Stop #87
Sea Level

Sea level is the level of the sea's surface. This is a helpful way to show how high landforms like hills and valleys are.

Fun Fact

There are many places that are below sea level, like Death Valley in California.

Stop #88
Ridge

Ridges are long, narrow hilltop ranges, with two sloping sides meeting at the top. Ridges can vary in size, from small hills to massive mountain ranges.

Fun Fact

Ridges can also be seen deep underwater, like the Mid-Atlantic Ridges, illustrated here, which span the entire Atlantic Ocean!

Stop #89
Reef

A reef is a ridge of rock that lies just beneath the surface of natural water. Reefs are known to harbor vast ecosystems of life, such as coral and fish.

Fun Fact

An underwater ridge can also be known as a shoal.

Stop #90
Spit

A spit (or sandspit) is a narrow landform that sticks into the ocean. Usually, they appear where shores change direction.

Fun Fact

Spits are even narrower than capes. They can even be classified as sandbars.

Stop #91
Seaport

A seaport is a small town or city with a harbor for ships to pick up or drop off cargo.

Stop #92
Savanna

A savanna is a grassy plain in the subtropical region with relatively few trees.

Fun Fact

The African Savanna is a popular savanna, being the home of creatures like lions and zebras.

Stop #93
Steppe

A steppe is an area of flat, unforested grassland. There are hardly any trees except for around lakes and rivers.

Stop #94
<u>Slope</u>

A slope is the gradual elevation of land over a distance. It can be gradual and slow, or steep and intense.

Fun Fact

The slope at the edge of a continental shelf is called the continental slope.

Stop #95
Snowline

A snowline is the elevated part of a mountain or cliff that's high enough for snow to start forming. It's that white section seen on mountains.

Fun fact

There is a similar line that marks the limit where trees stop growing, called the timber line.

Stop #96
<u>Tableland</u>

A tableland is a broad, high piece of land.

Fun fact

Tablelands are commonly seen around mesas.

Stop #97
Swamp

A swamp is an area of low-lying, uncultivated ground where water collects. The illustration here is a mangrove swamp.

Fun fact

Swamp can be both a noun and a verb, both involving lots of water in a low-lying place.

Stop #98

Tundra

A tundra is a vast, flat, treeless region of land that spans the Arctic.

Fun fact

The dirt in the tundra is consistently frozen making it difficult for things like trees to grow in it.

Stop #99
Sea

A sea is a large body of water that covers a significant part of the world. Although it is often confused with an ocean, a sea is much smaller, usually surrounded by land.

Fun fact

What is seen here is a topography of the Bering Sea. A topography is a detailed representation of landforms on a map.

Stop #100
<u>Taiga</u>

Taigas are biomes characterized by coniferous forests that are in the northern region. Coniferous forests are so named because of the coniferous trees that grow there.

Fun fact

Taigas are known to be snowy, however there are also taigas that are swampy.

Stop #101
Timber

Timber is wood from trees that has been cut down for use.

Stop #102
Tunnel

A tunnel is a passage made to get through something. They can be underground, in buildings, or even through trees.

Fun fact

Some trees are large enough to have tunnels you can drive through with a car!

Stop #103
Terrace

A terrace is a step-like landform made of flat or gently sloping geometric platforms separated by a steep slope. These slopes are called scarps.

Fun fact

Terraces can be both natural and artificially made, with the latter being used for things like rice farming!

Stop #104
Upstream / Downstream

Upstream is the action of going against the current of a stream or moving water source. Downstream is the opposite, going with the current.

Fun fact

Salmon are famously known for being fish that swim upstream.

Stop #103
Tributary

A tributary is a smaller river that connects to a much larger river or lake.

Fun fact

The Mississippi River has about 250 tributaries connected to it.

Stop #106
Volcano

Volcanos are hills or mountains with a crater on top. This crater leads to a vent that stretches deep under the earth, which can release hot magma and ash.

Fun fact

Despite how dangerous volcanos are, they help create fertile ground for plants.

Stop #107
Wave

A wave is a raised mass of water on the surface of the water, especially the sea. When waves are high enough, they arch over and crash. At that point, they are called breakers.

Fun fact

Like currents, waves aren't only in water. They are in air, the ground, and even sound.

Stop #108
Waterfall

A waterfall is a cascade of water falling from a steep incline such as a cliff.

Fun fact

Some waterfalls, like Angel Falls, are high enough that all their water simply evaporates to mist before touching the ground.

Stop #109
Whirlpool

A whirlpool is a spiral current of water with a depression in the middle. Usually, a whirlpool is a sign that there are two conflicting currents, or a drainage of water.

Stop #110
Woods

Woods are areas that are covered by trees. The key difference between woods and forests is that woods are smaller.

Stop #111
Valley

A valley is the low land between mountains or cliffs. Sometimes there is a river or even small forest or plains in the middle.

Fun fact

There are many synonyms for valley such as vale, dale, or basin.

Index

Altitude 2
Archipelago 1
Arm 4
Atoll 3
Bank 5
Basin 6
Bay 8
Bayou 7
Beach 9
Bluff 10
Bog 11
Brink 12
Canal 13
Canyon 14

Cape 15
Cave 16
Cavern 17
Channel 19
Chasm 18
Cinder Cone 20
Cliff 21
Continental Shelf 23
Continent & Country 22
Cove 24
Crags 25
Crater 26
Creek 27
Cultivated Land 28

Current	29
Dale	30
Dam	31
Dell	33
Delta	32
Desert	34
Dike	36
Dune	35
Earth	37
Estuary	39
Fall Line & Elevation	38
Field	40
Fjord	42
Foothill	43
Ford	41
Forest	45
Glacier	44
Gorge	46
Gulch	47
Gulf	48
Harbor	51
Headland	49
Hill	50
Iceberg	52
Inlet	56
Irrigated Land	57
Island	53
Isthmus	54
Junction	58
Jungle	55
Knobs & Knolls	59
Lake	61
Latitude & Longitude	60
Levee	63
Locks	62
Marsh	65
Meadow	64
Mesa	66
Mine	67
Moor	70
Mountain	68
Mountain Range	69
Mouth	71
Natural Resource	72
Oasis	75
Ocean	73
Pasture	76
Peninsula	74

Piedmont & Pass	77
Pier	81
Plain	79
Plateau	78
Pond	80
Rapids	82
Reef	89
Ridge	88
River	83
River Mouth	84
Sandbar	86
Savanna	92
Sea	99
Sea Level	87
Seaport	91
Shore	85
Slope	94
Snowline	95
Spit	90
Steppe	93
Swamp	97
Tableland	96
Taiga	100
Terrace	103
Timber	101
Tributary	105
Tundra	98
Tunnel	102
Upstream /Downstream	104
Valley	111
Volcano	106
Waterfall	108
Wave	107
Whirlpool	109
Woods	110

Sources and recommended materials

- languages.oup.com
- education.nationalgeographic.org
- www.dictionary.com
- www.britannica.com
- Luhr F. James, "DK Smithsonian Earth the Definitive Visual Guide." New York, 2013

Milton Keynes UK
Ingram Content Group UK Ltd.
UKHW050239280524
443233UK00003B/31